Hal•Leonard
Classical
PLAY-ALONG™

Volume 20

Ludwig van
BEETHOVEN
(1770-1827)

Two Romances for Violin, Op. 40 in G and Op. 50 in F

The Hal Leonard Classical Play-Along™ series allows you to work through great classical works systematically and at any tempo with accompaniment.

Tracks 2 and 7 on the CD demonstrate the concert versions of each piece. After tuning your instrument to Track 1 you can begin practicing. Using the Amazing Slow-Downer technology included on the CD, you can adjust the recording to any tempo you like without altering the pitch. (Note that when using Amazing Slow-Downer, the CD will stop after each track instead of playing continuously.)

- Track No. ☐1☐ – tuning notes
- Track numbers in circles ◯ – concert version
- Track numbers in diamonds ◆ – play-along version

CONCERT VERSION

Alexey Bruni, Violin

Russian Philharmonic Orchestra Moscow

Boris Perrenoud, Conductor

ISBN 978-1-4234-8894-1

HAL•LEONARD®
CORPORATION
7777 W. BLUEMOUND RD. P.O. BOX 13819 MILWAUKEE, WI 53213

In Australia Contact:
Hal Leonard Australia Pty. Ltd.
4 Lentara Court
Cheltenham, Victoria, 3192 Australia
Email: ausadmin@halleonard.com.au

Visit Hal Leonard Online at
www.halleonard.com

ROMANCE IN G MAJOR

for Violin and Orchestra, Op. 40

L. van Beethoven (1770–1827)

3

ROMANCE IN F MAJOR

for Violin and Orchestra, Op. 50

⑦

L. van Beethoven (1770 - 1827)

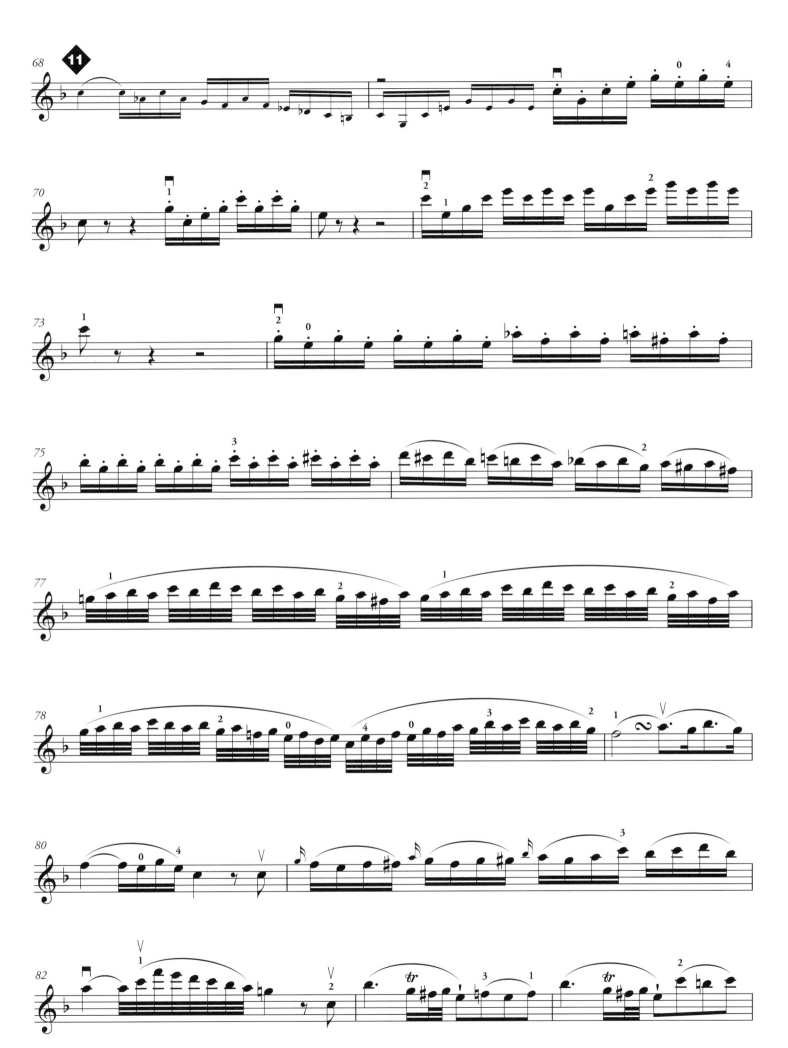

calando